This book was written on Dja Dja Wurrung Country. Generations of Jaara people in the custodianship of Dja Dja Wurrung land lovingly cared for this Country in a way that meant all beings were in balance and harmony. Their vision carried beyond their present time into future generations. These plans were decimated by the colonisers, who destroyed that visionary wisdom that infused the earth. With deep respect for First Nations People and sorrow for what has been taken, I tread as lightly as I can with every act. Always was, always will be.

YOU'LL BE A WONDERFUL PARENT

ADVICE and ENCOURAGEMENT for RAINBOW FAMILIES of ALL KINDS

JASPER PEACH

WITH ILLUSTRATIONS BY QUINCE FRANCES

Hardie Grant

BOOKS

TO YOU AND YOUR FAMILY – MAY THE PATH SHINE BRIGHT
FOR ALL OF US. I THANK YOU AND I'M IN AWE OF YOU.

TO WINSOME AND MICHAEL – WHO TOLD ME I COULD
DO ANYTHING, AND SHOWED ME IT WAS TRUE BY
NEVER WAVERING.

TO TRACEY AND OUR GOLDEN LIGHTS – THANK YOU FOR
BEING MY FAMILY. I LOVE YOU MORE THAN WORDS
OR SOUNDS OR CRAFT SUPPLIES COULD EVER CONVEY.

J.P.

FOR MY FAMILY, WHOSE LOVE MAKE MY WORK AND
PARENTING POSSIBLE.

Q.F.

CONTENTS

HEY YOU

I see you there, sitting outside the majority, away from the place where most family-centric focus lands. I was once where you are, in the strange and uncertain place before my baby was born. Five years down the track, my wife and I are ensconced in the most exquisite village.

I am trans, non-binary, disabled, and my two kids call me Mama Jay. I'm here for you and I want you to know you are going to be a wonderful parent.

You can do this.

Advice is a funny thing, and something I usually shy away from providing unless specifically asked, other than the key imperative to nap as much as possible before your baby arrives (I still look back fondly on those afternoon sleeps with my beautiful pregnant wife and our two dogs).

But I digress. **WHEN IT COMES TO WISDOM, I BELIEVE IT IS COMPRISED OF EQUAL PARTS EXPERIENCE AND HUMILITY.** I want to extend an invitation: that you read some encouraging words and anecdotes about the times before, during and after a baby arrives, and see where they land with your lived experience. Those first steps into the parenting unknown as a member of the LGBTIQA+ community will bring you to a road less travelled for the majority, but you are far from alone.

Before we dive in, I wish to acknowledge that language is a rapidly evolving ecosystem – and so it should be. There are many names given to us, and while some of them fit wonderfully, others feel more like sand rubbing in your gumboots.

In my mind, we are alphabet soup: a heady mix of stories that enrich all who come into our orbit. The LGBTIQA+ community is as diverse as humanity itself and, although it's a mouthful to say, it is essential that we are consistently inclusive of all people to whom it calls, that the more privileged give a leg up to the overlooked, and – most especially – that respect is given to all members of the team.

As time marches on, new terminology enters the lexicon and new identities are defined and lived. Some parts of language are laid to rest, then resurrected as needed. The singular they/them which I myself use as my pronouns originally appeared in literature in 1375 and was regularly in use for centuries before and after this time. If you see language in these pages that is out of date, I look forward to updating it in future editions.

WHEREVER YOU PLACE YOURSELF IN OUR COMMUNITY, WHOEVER AND WHEREVER YOU ARE, THIS BOOK IS FOR YOU.

You may find yourself at any of the myriad stages on the road to parenthood (birthing or otherwise). You may need the words in these pages today, or you may metaphorically tuck them away, whether it's in memory, heart storage, or quite literally in that drawer with all the bits and bobs you're not sure where to put, but think will probably come in handy someday.

You may be a same-sex couple, a queer solo parent, a cisgender male and female couple where one or both of you identify as part of the LGBTIQA+ community, a couple with one or two trans, genderqueer, non-binary or genderfluid humans. You may be co-parenting as a group of parents and caregivers with some or all of you being part of the queer community; you may be in a triad, foursome, moresome, or any configuration under the sun, and indeed the rainbow, if I may be permitted a moment of indulgence.

You may be working with a surrogate to bring a baby into your family, or be a person with a womb whose partner also has a womb and is carrying your shared child. You may be the person who is pregnant and preparing to birth your child.

It is essential to celebrate the people in our community who become caregivers in other scenarios. Many of us come out later in life, our heteronormative relationships replaced by queer or same-sex ties, and children from those formative family structures gain significant others to look to for love and guidance in their parents' new partner/s.

I also wish to acknowledge that not all people in our community have the desire or ability to become parents or caregivers. Being child-free by choice is just one of life's many well-travelled pathways, and there are countless people in the LGBTIQA+ community who face pitying assumptions and pressure to procreate. Just because it's possible doesn't mean we have to do it.

While our families are as varied as the people who comprise them, one thing is common: our children are most often created with intention, hope, careful planning and loving devotion. That is such a beautiful foundation to build a family upon.

YOUR VERY ESSENCE, AND THE FACT YOU HAVE – AGAINST ALL ODDS – ARRIVED AT THIS MOMENT JUST AS YOU ARE, TELLS ME THAT YOU HAVE WHAT IT TAKES FOR THIS LIFE. Bringing children into it is, at once, the most ordinary thing in the world, and also a life-exploding phenomenon.

But being part of this rainbow community means you have reflected on who you are and how you define yourself. That takes great thought and consideration: acknowledging and accepting your identity through coming out first to yourself, and potentially to others, requires courage and an understanding of what makes you who you are. There is no part of this that is a coincidence, or even a happy accident. Identifying as any flavour of queer is a sacred and truth-seeking path, just like becoming a parent.

Once we decided to bring a baby into our family, I was bowled over every time I saw a human. Every single person was born! They all had parents! Why is nobody stopping and exclaiming in wonder about this situation, every single moment of every single day? This is the magic – details rendered significant and appreciated anew that are too often assumed commonplace.

If you're like me, you never saw the family you're in the process of making represented in your community, mainstream media, or even creative outlets. Can you imagine being surrounded by families like yours when you were growing up? The LGBTIQA+ community is a marginalised minority that is under-represented and overlooked. That is changing day by day for the better, and I'm here to add to the chorus applauding and seeing us as we are. Diverse and powerful, courageous and real. It may not be your intention, or even your wish, but this is a life of activism. Simply bringing your baby into the world adds scope to the field of collective vision and is an epically positive and population-changing outcome.

THIS BOOK IS FOR YOU, TO SAY THANK YOU AND TO - IDEALLY - LEND A HELPING HAND IN THE WOOLLY, WONDERFUL AND WILD TIMES AHEAD. It is not intended as a comprehensive guide to conception or adoption, nor can it speak to the full kaleidoscope of experiences across our community of many colours. Rather, I offer it as a handbook of hope for anyone embarking on the path to parenthood, drawing on my own lived experience, and some anecdotal evidence gathered in the process from other queer parents.

If your voice is missing from these pages, I welcome the humbling opportunity to receive your parenting stories in return. We are, if nothing else, a Village People.

CONCEPTUAL
THINKING

hether you are doing this solo, with a friend or partner, or with multiple co-parents, I bet your family story has had or will require some fairly intentional action. With ever-shifting rules, laws and possibilities when it comes to creating a baby, you're likely to have multiple options around how to get this party started.

There are many questions and a lot of discussions to be had, with yourself and/or with others.

Where are the parts you need to make this baby coming from? Do you have an egg? How about sperm? Do you have a place for this kiddo to gestate? How do you make these decisions, and what implications do they have for this child and, indeed, for your family, your community and the world? What are your values? If you are in a partnership, is it important that you agree on every single aspect? How do you feel, and then react, when conflict arises? How are you funding this undertaking? How many times will you try? What could your other options look like?

That's all before you've even reached the starting blocks. You cannot cover everything all at once, and you can only do your best.

PACE YOURSELF: THIS IS A BIG DEAL.

A strange phenomenon that arises when a baby becomes part of the conversation is that people filter your experiences through their own lived lens. Diversity gives way to dogma, and there can be an unwelcome sense of ownership around the 'right' or 'wrong' way to do family, pregnancy, birth, breast and chest feeding, along with all the parenting rules you never knew were up for discussion

THE OUTSIDE WORLD MAY THINK THEY KNOW WHAT FAMILY MEANS, BUT YOUR FAMILY IS COMPLETELY UNIQUE AND YOURS TO DEFINE. Creating it takes energy, and you are absolutely entitled to conserve yours, and not spend it filling the gaps in other people's self-education.

Consider this your official permission.

We are conditioned to be polite, to not make anyone feel uncomfortable, often at the expense of our own agency and ownership of our hard-won identities. Correcting takes courage: not only do you have to deal with the other person's discomfort, but too often their reaction also shifts the onus to helping them feel better after their misstep.

You can choose whether or not to engage in a discussion, but it is never your sole responsibility to educate. A wealth of information is available to the wider community at the swipe of a smartphone.

I try to give people the benefit of the doubt and, when feeling robust, to offer my perspective on how their words felt as I absorbed them. The outcome can go either way, and in some unimaginable directions too.

Contemplating parenthood can be a time of identity formation.

Sam (they/them) identifies as non-binary, transgender, genderqueer and transmasculine. Part of preparing to be a parent involved Sam truly understanding themselves, knowing that when the time came, they would be able to look their baby in the eye knowing they weren't hiding anything from themselves or anyone else. Coming out as transgender in the workplace when Sam was newly pregnant was a celebratory and supportive experience.

Whichever way you choose to roll the dice I want you to know – to be reassured – that your identity is only enhanced, not diminished, through becoming a parent. The opportunity to express yourself and all facets of your sexuality and/or gender may be limited, particularly in medical settings, but it's important to remember that you are incredibly valid just as you are. **YOU ARE QUEER ENOUGH, BISEXUAL ENOUGH, PANSEXUAL ENOUGH OR TRANS ENOUGH**: this family is defined, affirmed and strengthened by your very you-ness, and that is a beautiful thing.

IT TAKES A VILLAGE TO RAISE A CHILD, OR SO THE SAYING GOES, AND THIS IS TRUE, TOO, OF THE CREATION OF OUR FAMILIES. There are often many moving and mutable parts, people who selflessly help to balance the scales of injustice. Egg donors, sperm donors and surrogates give of their own bodies, time and energy, releasing into the ether an element of themselves that they possibly, even likely, will have no further contact with or influence over. Some of these donations are anonymous; depending on policy, your child may be informed of their donor's identity when they come of age.

In our case, we opted for a known donor. He was someone who knew being a parent was not for him, but he could see that it was for us and couldn't think of any reason not to help, despite being honest and saying he didn't know how he would feel when our baby was born.

It is truly humbling when your family can be formed with this incredible generosity.

If you're forging ahead as a couple with two uteruses at your disposal, there's the task of deciding who will be the birthing and non-birthing party. If you are two people who identify as women, you may face insensitively worded questions such as 'Who will be the mum?' or even worse 'Who's the real mum?'

Ditto similarly invasive and reductive questions in a dynamic of two dads, and for adoptive or surrogate couples, who confront not only a labyrinthine and at times hostile bureaucracy, but the assumptions and preconceptions of a world where provenance and biology rule supreme.

Philosophical notions of what the word 'real' even means aside, this kind of discourse can chip away at your sense of self. **YOU ARE BOTH PARENTS.**

Huey (he/him) and Joseph (he/him) adopted their son when he was five years old. Joseph has always wanted children, whereas Huey took longer to reach a place of readiness, and learned to parent as he went. Neither felt the biological urge to create children, and knew that adoption was the right pathway for them.

Adoption by same-sex couples was still fairly new in 2008, and although they were never discouraged, there was always a feeling of being back of the queue – and not just because of their sexuality. At the time, Huey's Asian heritage seemed to disqualify them from being matched with many children. There wasn't any overt discrimination, but they sensed there were unspoken reasons why the adoption agency staff put less effort in with them than other couples.

Being part of a social group for LGBTIQA+ adopters and their children provided great support.

There are endless configurations that comprise a rainbow family, and **THE CONSCIOUS CHOICE TO EMBARK ON SINGLE PARENTHOOD IS A COURAGEOUS ONE WORTHY OF ACKNOWLEDGEMENT AND SUPPORT.**

When Alex (she/her) returned from overseas visibly pregnant she was met with cooing condescension, in the form of people asking who 'the father' was, at chance encounters and social gatherings. Eventually, Alex posted on social media asking friends and loved ones to stop asking about something that wasn't relevant to her growing family, which comprised herself as a queer woman, and the baby in utero. There was nothing missing, and to imply that there was felt unimaginative and frustrating.

It's easy to get swept up in the excitement of a potential baby, but it is also important to do your research about the financial, legal and legacy implications of how you choose to bring a baby into your family.

For example, you may not be eligible in some jurisdictions for government-funded parental payments and childcare subsidies if you opt for home insemination because, even though your donor will not be undertaking a parenting role, they would be considered financially responsible. Know your legal status – will you be on the birth certificate? What will happen to any excess embryos in storage in the event of separation or death? Will you formalise expectations and limitations of a donor or surrogacy arrangement in writing? What will it cover? If you are fostering or adopting, do you know your rights and obligations? **ARE YOU ACROSS THE RELEVANT LOCAL LAWS AND REGULATIONS?** Have you created or updated your will?

It's a lot to take in, and there are many organisations and individuals out there working pro bono who can help you sweat the small and not-so-small print.

FINDING THE RIGHT MEDICAL CARE CAN BE VERY DIFFICULT.
It can feel a bit strange – even frightening – walking into a space where you are the minority and are there seeking healthcare.

In my family, we opted for IVF and were in the privileged position to have the means to do so. After a few missteps with the first IVF clinic having trouble with locating our files, and doing ridiculous things like calling two days before commencing a cycle to say my beautiful wife was too hefty to undergo treatment and would need to diet-shake her way to being a more fertile size, we found a private IVF doctor who we could see exclusively for a tiny extra cost. That was all it took to get continuous care from someone we got to know and trust.

The best way to find these doctors is to ask people in your community who have babies; someone will have a name to pass on to you. If you're lucky like us, they'll make a call on your behalf, and the personal connection makes everything possible. It goes without saying that things shouldn't be this way; everyone deserves excellent care regardless of who they know.

Your family may look like a straighty-180 suburban catalogue dream, but when one or both of you lay claim to any of the letters in the alphabet soup, there is a terrible sense of erasure that can creep in.

A LOT OF THE SYSTEMS WE LIVE WITHIN LET US DOWN, sometimes in ways as simple as the options available in a drop-down menu. I remember not knowing how to answer the question of whether I was the primary parent: did they mean the birthing parent? In our family we were equal. When a trans man sees a birthing staff member and they list their gender as male, many of the routine check-ups and procedures during their gestation are no longer on the menu.

Medical erasure and discrimination are worse when your identity sits at an intersection.

Most people in the LGBTIQA+ community have enough wherewithal to check our privilege. We know what it is to be marginalised. The fertility industry is just that: an industry, part of a capitalist system that prioritises profit over empowerment and care. There need to be affordable, equitable and accessible pathways to reproductive technology so that it's not just possible for some of us. Equality will remain elusive as long as some of us are excluded and left behind.

If you feel that you can, a quick email to a feedback address can go a long way. It can also help you to release some of the grief involved, knowing that you've taken a step to protect others in your position from similar experiences in future. But you are under no obligation to retraumatise yourself to fix a system that is not necessarily made with you in mind.

For every instance you're lectured – authoritatively – on the way things are, there will be an opportunity to make a decision and definition for yourself.

I'll give you an example. A long time ago, my partner and I sat around a table with a person who we thought would be our donor, and we all agreed that the donor would be like an uncle to the baby we hoped would be born. Across the three people involved in that discussion were three completely different definitions of the word 'uncle'. For me it was someone I heard mentioned every year or two, and who I rarely saw, if ever. For my partner, an uncle was someone who was respected, and often popped in on weekends to visit. And for our prospective donor, an uncle was someone who took you away on holidays multiple times a year. You can imagine how confusing it was, after all agreeing to the uncle role, to later discover those wildly variable ideals.

But this is one of the great things about untangling prescribed definitions and seeing what works – **YOU CAN FORGE NEW UNDERSTANDINGS WITHIN YOUR FAMILY UNIT, WHATEVER CONFIGURATION THAT HOLDS.**

Whatever the process, bringing a baby into your family can be difficult. It's a journey that will stretch you to your limits, and **IT'S VITAL TO REMAIN CONNECTED TO AND COMMUNICATING WITH WHOEVER IT IS THAT YOU'RE ON THE ROAD WITH.**

Conception via assisted reproductive technology is forging your family through fire. The process and its impact on everyone involved is not to be underestimated. My wife bore the physical and hormonal brunt of IVF, and we clutched one another for dear life throughout. Along the way we faced police checks, blood screening for both of us (with no clarification offered as to why my blood was needed too), and counselling to determine if we would even be approved, both for us as a couple and for our donor. We were labelled geriatric, bariatric, socially and psychologically infertile, and countless other derisive things that have fallen through the cracks of memory. It was a marathon. I injected the person I love in the belly every morning, hurting her for what felt like years. I wept on long drives to our local capital city (where great IVF treatment was available) because the hope was sticking in my throat and I couldn't see or feel anything else.

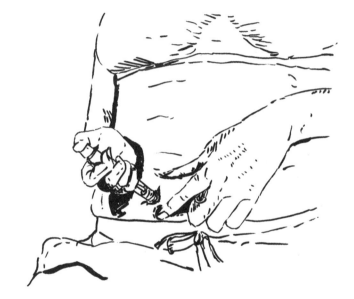

During this time, I found it impossible to give much to anyone other than my wife, to hold the woes of friends or family like I usually have the capacity for. I knew I needed to safeguard every shred of energy I had as we were preparing to become a fledgling family of three humans (plus two dogs, one cat and multiple chickens). It was important to gently let people know this, rather than simply removing my dependable presence in their lives. Once I explained, people generally understood, and it was positive, proactive preparation for life with a baby, where everything – and everyone – else takes a back seat. Giving to others is only possible when the people in your immediate circle are safe, loved and have what they need. I had never experienced that before, but I felt it viscerally in every fibre of my being. It was a primal urge.

My wife let me process things in my own unique way. She knows my peaks and troughs well, and allowed me to have my moments. I held her or gave her space as needed, and did my best to be thoughtful about her experiences and how to support her in the ways that counted. Being the person that not only shows up for others but can prioritise care for yourself demonstrates that you will do what it takes to stay strong and present.

Although we needed our space, this period was also incredibly lonely. Many non-conventionally aspiring parents know this isolation well, whether it's the legs-up-the-wall anxiety of insemination, the nail-biting weeks between surrogate check-ups for news, or the seemingly interminable hurry-up-and-wait bureaucracy of adoption or fostering.

WHILE IT'S IMPORTANT TO HAVE BOUNDARIES, DON'T FORGET THAT YOUR COMMUNITY ARE THERE. I asked my wife's nearest and dearest to send me something to bolster her through the incredibly gruelling hormonal treatments, day surgery, invasive tests and ultimately endless waiting ahead. Getting my crafternoon on, I used these to create a shimmering mobile of affirmations to hang above our bed, for her to see and feel held and encouraged by.

For prospective single parents preparing to welcome a new addition, you may wish to have a special person or a trusted group of people to be key supports as you traverse the ups and downs. What matters most is that you give yourself space to have your needs met.

Daring to dream can be such a leap of faith: a tender place to find yourself when things are completely out of your control. Whichever way you plan to bring a baby into your family, everything could go just as you imagined, or you could be faced with zigs when you expected zags, the blueprint gone belly-up in ways you could never have anticipated.

Phoebe (she/her) is a single mother and a bisexual intersex woman. Phoebe doesn't have a uterus or ovaries, which means she has never menstruated and is unable to carry a child. Her experience of growing up intersex was one of secrecy, stigma and shame. Even as a child, Phoebe knew she wanted to be a parent, and adopting her daughter in 2009 was more than she ever hoped for. She has since separated from her daughter's father but is enjoying being single mother to a teenager, fostering resilience and an ability to accept and celebrate herself that makes her a better parent.

KNOW THAT ALL YOUR EXPERIENCES CAN HELP TO MAKE YOU A BETTER PARENT.

Carve out time to process it all as you go. Rest, nutrition (including comfort food, obviously), moving your body, debriefing, creating – whatever works to anchor you to your most grounded centre, as the sands shift beneath your feet.

Being told what to make peace with or why fortune did or did not favour you can be the most crushing blow. There are as many complex belief systems as there are people, and when – not if – others try to gift you theirs, it's ok to turn away and seek your own answers inside yourself. **THINK OF BELIEFS LIKE SHOES: IF THEY'RE NOT COMFORTABLE AND YOU DON'T FEEL GOOD FROM YOUR HEAD TO YOUR TOES WHEN WEARING THEM, THEY'RE NOT FIT FOR THE PATH YOU ARE FOLLOWING.**

You are trying very hard to achieve something that is ultimately luck of the draw. It's like falling in love: impossible to force, a game of chance, and fraught with emotions like grief, fear, hope and joy. If you are lucky and the statistical fair winds favour your plotted course, it can be a challenge to let go of the terror that you may yet be becalmed. What matters is that you are a person of worth, no matter the fickle seas.

PREPARING FOR ARRIVAL

aiting for a child to join you will be a period of your life like no other. Putting pen to paper, setting up an email address, recording yourself via audio or video to begin the telling of a shared story – all these methods can help you process and acknowledge what's happening in your inner world in that liminal space.

While a baby is growing, there are various yardsticks the endeavour is held up against. There are the days and weeks, scans and appointments. The fruit series is a particularly good one – the foetus is the size of a watermelon seed, a lemon, an avocado, a honeydew melon. There are endless opportunities for cute photographs to document this time using groceries as props.

IF I MAY, A PIECE OF IRON-CLAD ADVICE: DO NOT REVEAL YOUR DUE DATE. You will be inundated with text messages, phone calls, gifs and memes from people telling you to hurry up. It will not be funny, or fun, or cool. It will feel like pressure. My advice? Be a bit airy fairy about it; say late in the month or early the next.

Your baby doesn't know their due date and has no interest in sticking to a schedule. Keep that secret squirrel to yourselves and revel in your little family secret.

People seem to feel an insatiable need to ask a pregnant person what they're having. I quite liked responding that a baby goat would be born any day now, and how thrilled we were about all the potential bars of soap their milk could produce.

You may be less obnoxious than me, but the obsession with the genitals of unborn babies strikes me as a bit crude, not to mention irrelevant.

THERE ARE MANY FAMILIES NOW RAISING THEIR CHILDREN GENDER-NEUTRAL, OFFERING SPACE AND TIME FOR THE CHILD TO DECIDE FOR THEMSELVES HOW THEY IDENTIFY. This also dilutes the fixed ways of interaction determined by gender markers. Can you imagine how different the world would be if all children assigned male at birth had been offered consistent nurturing and gentle care? The course of history would have been altered in ways I can't even begin to imagine.

Nayuka (they/them) is a Gunai/Kurnai, Gunditjmara, Wiradjuri and Yorta Yorta non-binary person, and Witt (they/he) is a white trans person. They are parents of twin toddlers and kinship carers for their niblings. They knew that they wanted to empower their kids to decide their own identity, so the babies have the pronouns they/them. Nayuka and Witt are also abolitionists, meaning they avoid violence in their home, including punishment or raised voices.

The twins were conceived using donor sperm from a close friend, in their second home-insemination attempt. Through a difficult pregnancy and birth, they received excellent care from their midwife, who also did some advocacy and pronoun education on their behalf for other staff at the hospital. They especially love how their Blak queer community have embraced their family and made this life possible.

During gestation, if you are not the person carrying and birthing your baby and you live with or support the person who is, it is essential that you know one thing: **IF IT FEELS TRUE TO THE BIRTHING PARENT, THAT'S ALL THAT MATTERS.** Have their back and support their feelings. Be it a changing sensitivity to food that emerges between an urgent, specific meal request and the serving of same, or a sense that someone is treating them badly, your first and most important job is to listen – silently, but with encouraging facial expressions. Then you must act accordingly. Fetch for them whatever they now want to eat, acknowledge that it must be very upsetting to feel this way about an interaction, and move on.

With you as their primary champion, trust will be established in a way it hasn't been needed before. You will both feel a new kind of vulnerability as you get closer to the birth of your baby, and both of you knowing that your feelings are valued and heard will make all the difference. Your team will be strengthened in the run-up to parenthood.

If you are the birthing parent, there may be a complex and contradictory set of emotions at play.

Pregnancy might be all soft focus and sweetness, child-bearing hips and hormonal highs. But you may struggle with the loss of bodily autonomy, or find the gender disconnect dysphoric, particularly if you were someone who had previously been on the more androgynous-presenting, non-binary, masc or trans end of the spectrum. This will only be reinforced by the insistent imposition of social pressures and opinions.

Always come back to who you are, that your identity and sense of self is valid and true. Lean on your closest circle for support and encouragement.

If you are a non-birthing parent (who may or may not have the necessary bodily apparatus to birth a baby), you may have mixed feelings during this time: wishing it was you, relief that it isn't, or both. Your baby may be growing in a body far from where you're located, or in the care of others while you lay the foundations for their home. **THE MOST IMPORTANT THING TO KNOW IS THAT YOU ARE THIS BABY'S PARENT. THEY WILL LOVE YOU SO FIERCELY IT WILL FORCE YOU TO REIMAGINE THE DEFINITIONS OF DEVOTION AND FAMILY.** Although it feels distinctly possible in the pre-birth times that your child will relate to you differently, please be assured that they know who you are and feel the connection from the very moment they attain personhood.

While our baby was growing, I booked in to get a tattoo on my right inner forearm of a pinecone (a symbol of nature and science, as well as love – we were married under a massive pine tree). I wanted to mark the time with a physical experience for my own body as I wasn't growing the baby inside mine.

As we walk the unique journey to parenthood, there can be the drip-drip-dripping of small experiences that, at the time, feel silly to make a fuss over. But the accumulation of microaggressions is very real, and I want you to know that your feelings are valid.

Lisa (she/her) had never minded, in the past, that everyone assumed she was straight, but as a pregnant woman, automatically passing as heterosexual felt like a betrayal to her wife. She would correct people when they referred to her husband or the father of the baby, and they were genuinely mortified and would always apologise, but it would happen again and again. Lisa loved being pregnant, but suddenly it seemed like the very act was masking who she really was.

There are countless such examples of misunderstanding or falsely placed judgement. The look you get from another person when holding your partner's hand in a waiting room or attending birthing classes solo – these instances all matter. They are, in isolation, mere drops, but they form a vast and endless ocean and have the potential to chip away at your inner strength.

Do whatever you need to do to get through that moment and emerge ready for the inevitable next encounter.

Some ways I've found useful in dealing with microaggressions include: yelling at the sky, chatting with a friend who has lived experience of a similar situation, writing articles, eating chocolate until my feelings go away, counselling, more chocolate, crying, baking lovely things and sharing them so a positive feeling overtakes the negative. As one of the books I read to my kids says, **IT'S NORMAL TO FEEL ANGRY BUT IT'S NEVER OK TO HURT SOMEONE ELSE BECAUSE YOU DO.**

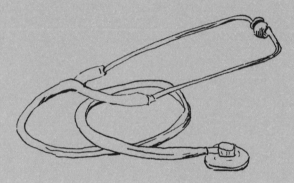

Hospitals and other medical spaces are busy places, but adequate care – including addressing people correctly – is a bare minimum at the most vulnerable time of a person's life. There are myriad organisations and individuals who provide workplace training to ensure staff are up to speed around inclusive language and practice, and there's no excuse in this day and age for falling short.

I am all about feedback and clear communication, but even I bow out most of the time where my family is involved. It can be exhausting or exhilarating to push for change, depending on an endless configuration of factors, chief among which is how much sleep you're getting. **IF SOMEONE CROSSES A LINE, IT'S NOT YOUR JOB TO EDUCATE THEM, AND IT'S PERFECTLY ACCEPTABLE TO ASK FOR ANOTHER MIDWIFE, DOCTOR OR NURSE.**

A celebration prior to birth may occur, and this can be a golden opportunity to reinvent the wheel. (Don't even get me started on gender reveal parties and how problematic they are.)

Sometimes people don't want to overstep and organise something on your behalf, and it's important to let your friends know if you'd like to celebrate with them. Nobody is obliged to have a baby shower with every friend, colleague and distant relative on the planet, opening gifts from a prescribed list and playing a 'guess the melted chocolate bar in the nappy' game – though if you would love a celebration like this, have at it.

When our first child was nearly ready to be born, my wife was taken out for lunch by her childhood best friend, feted and showered with love. It was an intimate celebration and one that suited her perfectly; she's not one for crowds.

I felt teary and alone that afternoon and wondered where my celebration was. I was also going to be a mother, a parent, and I felt silly for wanting a fuss when I hadn't been the one whose body fed and housed our foetus, and I wasn't going to be the one doing the birthing. But I knew enough by then to honour my feelings and let them flow through me, and I gingerly, tenderly let a friend know how I felt. Within minutes a dinner had been organised with two close friends for the next night, both parents themselves whose children I had loved deeply and cared for so they could have the odd night or afternoon to themselves.

TOO OFTEN PEOPLE IN THE LGBTIQA+ COMMUNITY ARE EXCLUDED FROM RITUAL BECAUSE WE DON'T KNOW HOW TO SLOT OURSELVES INTO A SYSTEM THAT DOESN'T HAVE US IN MIND. You're allowed to do whatever feels right for you to mark this significant milestone.

There are a lot of decisions to make around a birth, and we won't go through all of them here, but I will share some of the things that we did, in case they are directly relevant or strike a chord.

Our first baby was born in a hospital and we had a magnificent doula navigating the ride. Doulas are people experienced in supporting people during birthing, and bring a much-needed reassuring air, along with additional skills such as acupuncture, massage and psychological training. We prioritised this as a part of our budget and were privileged to be able to do so. With medical settings often being stark and sterile, we found the support of a trusted and frankly beloved person was a hugely impactful step we could take towards a safe, empowered birth.

It can be comforting to bring in a number of items from home to the space where you're labouring and birthing, especially if you're not giving birth at home. An aromatic diffuser, salt lamp or soft furnishings such as familiar blankets or quilts can help dispel the medicalisation of a birth suite.

We made a stack of copies of our birth preferences (we thought the word 'plan' was a bit silly as we couldn't decide how things would unfold) and were clear that we were a couple, what our pronouns were, that the baby didn't have a father, that we were the parents, and what my partner's wishes were about pain relief, induction and monitoring. **IT HELPED TO SPELL IT ALL OUT BECAUSE IT GAVE US TIME TO REALLY THINK ABOUT WHAT IT ALL MEANT.**

I did also have the foresight to plan a little playlist for the moment of birth, and each of our children have their own collection of songs that will transport us right back to that room whenever we hear them.

No matter where your baby is born, their arrival is something you'll never forget. It is the moment in time where your heart and your family expand and become your new normal.

YOU WILL GO THROUGH AN UNTOLD NUMBER OF STAGES AS YOU GET CLOSER TO MEETING YOUR CHILD. Sometimes it takes so long that it feels like the agonising eighteenth hour of an international flight, so it's important for both of you to get some rest when it's appropriate to do so.

As a birthing parent there are the bodily shocks of labour's various stages, and a deep retreat to draw on internal reserves you never even knew that you had. Key to harnessing the physical waves is fostering and being able to trust in a safe, calm, private space where you can be completely vulnerable. In a world that can feel alien, even hostile when you are beyond the cishet binary, this is not something that will come without work and preparation, both inside and out.

As the non-birthing parent, I knew that in order to be the best supportive partner possible, I needed to also prioritise my own needs. This meant regularly stretching my body, staying hydrated and eating nourishing snacks (fresh raspberries and sliced cucumber and watermelon are great as they're hydrating as well, but you might also desperately need a chocolate bar or some salty crunchy chips).

It also meant having a support person of my own that I could call on any time during the process – whether to discuss a *Seinfeld* plot or to just say 'Agghahghghghhhgghhggh! There's going to be a baby and I'm going to be a parent!'

I remember feeling that we were here forever, in this strange limbo, and time didn't exist. When they told us our baby would meet us soon it was such a shock; a big part of me had forgotten there was a baby coming.

Nothing can prepare you for the moment you first meet your child.

Daniel (he/him) and his partner Nigel (he/him) worked with an egg donor and separate surrogate in Canada; this choice came down to the fact that Daniel's age would work against them with adoption, and surrogacy in Australia involved complex hoops, red tape and varying laws. Daniel describes the family unit being formed like magnets tightly connected with the force of love, even though their baby was growing on the other side of the world. Their surrogate was warm and kind and will always be a special person for their family. Daniel and Nigel both cried the moment they saw their son come blazing into the world. When they got to hold him, it was beautiful and surreal; he fit into their arms like he'd always been there.

I didn't know if I was allowed to touch our first child when they were weighing and checking them over, so I asked and the midwife said, 'Of course! This is your baby!' I held hands with my child and told them I loved them. The rest of the world fell away. **THE FEELING WAS SUCH SHEER RELIEF** – like cool water on a parched body, the reassurance that they're safe, everyone is safe, and we're all together here now, at last.

The shock is something that most parents experience, but for us – constituents of the rich alphabet soup – it's a double whammy. This was never a given, and now it's truly happening.

THE
BUBBLE

As a new parent, the main thing – your main job – is to love the baby, make sure they have enough milk to drink, and keep them at the optimal temperature. In the case of a newborn, the first three months are all about the baby's system learning to be in the open, with all the stimulus that brings; they don't really know what's going on other than that, and they still feel part of the birthing parent's body, which is a beautiful thing to support going into the fourth trimester. For fostering, adoptive or other stripes of new parent getting to know their special person down the track, those early days are just as formative and life-changing. A new shared world is explored and the shapes of one another become familiar.

People will give you instructions about how to feel in this time. It can be incredibly confronting when you're being instructed to enjoy the magic amid bleeding nipples, sleep deprivation and the aches and pains that come with holding a squirmy little bub. Feel whatever you're feeling and don't try to push any of it down. It's ok. You do you.

Please don't feel guilty if you find it mind-meltingly hard and a bit awful. In the early days, the gratitude and relief mixes with hypervigilance and lack of sleep. Your body can get a bit muddled, and your mind can do some pretty psychedelic stuff when you have the new full-time job of protecting a human baby. You're doing your best to keep a tiny defenceless person alive at a time when it feels like your skin has disintegrated, leaving you more exposed than you've ever felt in your life. Everything has new meaning; everything cuts right to the core. This isn't reserved just for the first few months: it can seem overwhelming as different stages and ages pass, and sometimes the feeling of it all being too much can lead to guilt.

The thing is, all of it is true. It is an incredible stroke of luck that you won – against all odds – the lottery of a baby joining your family, and it can overwhelm and drain you.

There's no need to turn away from any of these observations. The most frankly mind-blowing thing about becoming a parent for me has been how many opposing things have been true at the same time, and how often.

There is a common refrain among parents of wee kids: nobody can explain it to you, you'll only understand once you're in it. This is true, and what is also true is that **AT FIRST IT ALL FEELS IMPOSSIBLE – UNTENABLE – UNTIL LITTLE BY LITTLE YOU FIND YOUR RHYTHM.**

Keep holding on to that, through any patches of uncertainty, fear or exhaustion: you will find your feet. Being a parent is a new skill that builds on itself, like the strength in a muscle, or the ability to cook a recipe from memory – the more you do it, the more capable you become.

Breast and chest feeding is something you can do a lot of preparation for, or you can have a crack once bubs is on your chest. It could be an endlessly difficult and triggering process, or your baby could latch on and go for gold (and anywhere in between).

Even when breast or chest feeding happens relatively easily, the physical demand on the person supplying the milk can be a huge shock. Support, snacks, hydration and understanding are essential, for everyone involved.

Do not let anyone shame you for any part of how you feed your baby. Formula is great, breast and chest milk is great; sometimes pumping and nipple shields help, sometimes they don't. Be gentle with yourself, no matter what happens. **YOU ARE ALLOWED TO MAKE A DECISION TO CARE FOR YOUR BABY IN A WAY THAT'S LOVING TO THEM AND TO YOURSELF.**

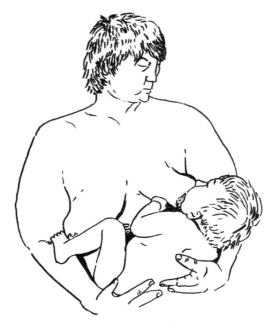

Lots of other advice will likely be flung in your direction, even and especially when no request has been made. For example, 'You'll be fine if you sleep when the baby sleeps,' or, 'Crying is just them trying to manipulate you.' Not all advice will be useful. Lots of it can get in the bin.

This also counts for advice you pay for, which often assumes that one approach will suit all families. For example, there is a huge industry built around the concept of sleep training. For some families, the haven of sleep school changes everything for the better. For other families, the typical advice has absolutely no place in your home. For Rae (they/them), parent to a non-neurotypical two-year-old, trying everything that they were instructed to did more harm than good, with most 'expertise' rooted in neurotypical assumptions. In Rae's view, the Western culture of sleep training is geared around 'fixing' babies who aren't broken, when there really needs to be more support for parents to care for their children, relying on their instincts.

I FOUND IT HELPFUL TO VISUALISE MYSELF AS TEFLON, LETTING ALL THE ADVICE THAT REALLY DIDN'T APPLY SLIDE OFF ME AND INTO THE ETHER.

Never will you feel more embraced by your community than when coming home as a newly extended family.

We were incredibly lucky to be fed by family and friends for a month after our first baby was born. Hot meals on the doorstep were so appreciated – and needed too. After our meal train ended, I went to visit the people who made us those delicious feasts and made sure to write down the recipes so I could pay some version of them forward in future. If people are far away and can't drop off a meal but would like to support you, you could accept gift vouchers for a meal-delivery service or nearby takeaway that you love.

One of the best things someone did was drop off a feeding pillow when I put a call out asking if anyone had a spare one. When I opened the door a crack and my friend saw me wild-eyed and heard the baby screaming, she passed over the pillow and a can of dry shampoo and said, 'I'll see you soon, you're doing great.' **THOSE SEEMINGLY SMALL THINGS ARE MAGNIFIED TENFOLD IN THE EARLY DAYS, AND MEAN SO MUCH.**

You might need more help than you anticipated.
When people offer, say yes, but don't feel guilty
about laying down boundaries. For example:
'Thank you it's so kind of you to offer to come and
hold the baby, but we're just bonding as a family for
now. It would be really helpful if you could drop off
some milk and chocolate biscuits some time when it
suits you.' Or: 'It's wonderful that you've made space
in your busy schedule to come and meet the baby but
it's their naptime right now. There is a heap of laundry
that needs folding and dishes to clean though, if you'd
really like to help.'

Whatever boundaries you feel are right, go with them.
This may vary daily, and that's fine too. Your baby will
change rapidly before your very eyes, so it's perfectly
natural that your feelings and needs will too.

When it's time to find your own way, when you start to cook for yourself and venture out a bit more, take it slow.

LEAVING THE HOUSE WITH YOUR BABY FOR THE FIRST TIME IS EPIC. We managed a walk around the block with the pram and the dogs a few weeks in and we had a huge debrief afterward, our eyes shining with wonder after reconnecting with the world outside the newborn bubble. Moving as a pack is like nothing else; make sure you take a moment to luxuriate in the pride you feel. You deserve it.

Notice what overwhelms you and see if there's anything you can do to break it down into smaller portions. If something feels great, do more of it! Prioritise things and people that fill your cup.

Whether it's at baby check-ups or new parents groups, feelings of erasure can continue, and you may not have it in you to push back.

While this kind of treatment is unacceptable, when you're in the vulnerable space of new parenthood it can feel like there is precious little energy to give to these battles. Your instinct to speak up for your own rights can feel diametrically opposed to the need for your partner and babies to receive proper care. In that moment it can feel like both outcomes are not possible. It is exhausting, demoralising and humiliating.

It is essential to keep front of mind, always, that your inherent worth is not contingent on the recognition of a system – or the people in it – designed not to see you.

Those early days when your child leans wholly on you and you feel the weight of them are like nothing else. There is the literal weight, which has its own impact physically, and then there is the presence of them, where before there was only the courage to dream. Seeing your children in your arms, and in the arms of other people who love them – for the first, tenth, hundredth time – is completely unlike any other experience.

AT TIMES, HAVING A CHILD IS LIKE THROWING A DECK OF CARDS INTO THE AIR: you have no idea how they'll fall, and it can feel like you're completely unanchored from the life you once knew. But one day in the not-too-distant future, you'll notice that the dust has settled. A quiet moment will sneak up on you, bringing peace of mind. That day will come, and you'll know that you can keep going.

FINDING YOUR GROOVE AS A FAMILY

Your family is hard won. It was never a given, and the protective urges will surge through your adrenals like nothing else. There is a part of your heart that is now outside in the world on its own, and though you are tasked with keeping this person safe, you won't be able to protect them forever.

What you can definitely do, however, is provide a nurturing foundation for security, a way for your child to have a strong sense of self so they know how to move through life with contentedness, pride and good humour. As much as you may feel a constant burning need to tell your children they are adored and protected, it is more likely to stick if you show your love and highlight their safety with every action.

There are so many opportunities for the perilous patriarchy to rear its ugly head when parenting is part of your life. But you are in an incredibly unique situation where you can decide every day where to place yourself. **YOUR FAMILY NEST CAN BE FEATHERED WITH THE VALUES YOU CHOOSE; YOUR BOUNDARIES CAN BE LOVINGLY BUILT TOGETHER.**

Tell your babies who the rightful and traditional owners are of the land they were born and live on. Show them how to live gently and respectfully, in harmony with nature and the seasons. Celebrate difference; show your children that all people are worthy of love and exclusion has no place in your world. Live your values and expose societal hierarchies as nothing more than a fable undeserving of your participation. Demonstrate that family can be logical as well as biological.

Your family is a tender lump of clay, shaped over time to become your child's reality and the safe home base where they will learn about love and belonging.

Language matters, and it can seem to let us down at every turn if we let it. Cue the confusion from extended family when two parents identify as mum, dad or neither, or the predictable pearl-clutching when parents announce they plan to be referred to by first name, as though roles are created through hierarchical terminologies, not love.

Naming can be empowering, though, and fun too. There aren't universal words for parents who don't identify as mum or dad, but there are some pretty wonderful examples out there, like mop (my other parent), or the affectionate moppy. The perceived problem comes when moppy's child refers to their parent thus, and nobody knows, instinctively, who they are talking about. But your family is literally on your terms, and anecdotes abound of the eye-rolling child policing a stranger or teacher on their incorrect use of mummy/mama/moppy or any moniker in between.

MEANING IS MADE, NOT MERELY RECEIVED, AND RECLAIMING LANGUAGE CAN BE A FORM OF RECLAIMING YOURSELF. Your kids, and those who love them, can and will figure it out.

As you emerge more frequently from the love bubble, time with people outside your safe inner circle may feel too difficult to face. There may be occasions like church weddings and christenings where you see pamphlets in the foyer that deny your family's right to exist. The festive season may see you swept into gleaming palaces of rigid gender roles.

Your children will watch how you react as they become old enough to understand, and this will inform how they behave in challenging situations. Our kids are so connected to us that they can feel the air change when we're upset, even if we're smiling. Lead by example, demonstrating through your actions and words that you are deserving of kindness and respect. This includes being kind and respectful to the people in your life who lead a charmed heteronormative existence – there is no place for judgement in any direction.

But also know that it is more than ok to remove yourself from any situation in which you don't feel welcomed and comfortable.

And when you return to your bubble, let your close ones remind you that you are seen and valued – that you belong. Logical family rituals and gatherings can be incredibly powerful in bringing you back to your sense of self. Being othered doesn't get easier with frequency, but building in emotional scaffolding in this way ensures a smooth transition between your worlds.

YOU MAY GET A LOT OF (OFTEN INAPPROPRIATE) QUESTIONS AND EVEN STATEMENTS ABOUT YOUR FAMILY.

There will be those who understand, those who know they don't get it and show openhearted curiosity, and those who think they get it – but don't.

One early childhood educator repeatedly asked who birthed our baby and could never seem to retain the response, which was none of her business in the first place. Then there was the toy library volunteer who knew our donor and announced they 'knew the dad' of our child: our children don't have a dad, and to hear someone declaring they did was a huge shock.

Joey (he/him), a trans man, has been the primary carer for his five-year-old niece since she was thirteen months old. Joey's niece calls him Uncle, or Poo, and sometimes asks if she can call him Dad. Joey's mum lives close by and co-parents 40 per cent of the time so Joey can continue with his job, and the rest of the family – Joey's dad, younger brother and second sister – are all very present in his niece's life. Despite bureaucratic challenges tied to Joey's gender identity, it is an unexpected yet joyful family life.

Outside this bubble, however, Joey is met with insulting statements, including how it's so weird that he's found himself raising a super girly girl who loves dresses and pink. Implicit in these comments is the suggestion that Joey's trans agenda is to not celebrate his niece for all that she is, where – in reality – his sole intention is to show this child he loves unconditionally that anything she dreams of is possible.

My wife and I used to find ourselves unwittingly answering probing questions about private matters because we were so taken aback, we didn't know what else to do. We didn't want to be rude or off-putting, lest it reflect badly on our community. There was also a desire for our experience to be seen as it is: perfectly natural and commonplace.

So we rehearsed our answers, upholding kind but firm boundaries. We embraced the idea that we didn't have to be anyone's super-cool story at a dinner party and reminded one another that the specifics of our children's origin stories belong to our family, and that is perfectly fine to assert.

Sometimes a child might come into your life in an unorthodox way, perhaps at a time and in a manner unexpected, and there will be different parenting obstacles to navigate.

When Natty (she/her) and Tané (she/her) met on a lesbian dating app, Tané told Natty about her family in one of their earliest chats – she had a baby and two teenagers, as well as an older stepchild. After two years together, Natty moved in and had to work out how to slot herself into the rhythm of the household.

Tané had a system that planned out meals, transport, homework and laundry, extending to such details as who would clean the kitchen sink. The only issue? This system wasn't written down anywhere and was challenging for Tané to articulate because it was just hard-wired into her being. Natty started at the outer edges of family life, and gradually found her spaces to contribute, reassuring Tané that care could become a shared load, not a favour or 'babysitting'.

Because Tané's first experiences of child-rearing had been as a step-parent, she was able to alert Natty to potential landmines and tensions – and there were many. Natty can still feel isolated, anxious or left out at times. But through respectful communication and a shared parenting philosophy, Natty and Tané have overcome these obstacles to form a strong team, and the kids see Natty as a parent – not because they've been told to, but because she has earned their trust.

THERE ARE COUNTLESS QUEER STEPPARENTS WHOSE HEARTS EXPECTED TO FIND ONE ADULT TO LOVE, ONLY TO HAVE THAT FEELING MANY TIMES MAGNIFIED FOR THE CHILDREN THAT COME ALONG WITH THEM.

CAREGIVING DOES NOT HAVE TO BE SYNONYMOUS WITH COLOCATION, and only living part-time with your children does not make you any less of a parent.

Jesse (he/him) is a gay trans parental figure to the children of an old cisgender heterosexual friend, both of whom were conceived with donor sperm. Physical and mental health issues meant full-time parenting was not an option for Jesse, but he committed to co-parenting with the kids' mum, who he has been close with since adolescence. As birth partner, Jesse cut the umbilical cord for both kids, and was the first person to hold them. He began transitioning when their eldest child was born, and changed his name to Jesse when they were three. There was a brief period of adjustment which passed swiftly. The children know Uncle Jesse has a boyfriend and it's no big deal.

The family have an established routine where Jesse stays two days a week, helping with the school run, breakfast, swimming classes, excursions and reading. For them, it's about quality of time, not quantity.

PARENTING ALONE CAN BRING ITS OWN CHALLENGES.

Rebecca (they/them) is a single parent who identifies as biromantic lite and asexual. Rebecca finds it difficult to date, because there don't seem to be a lot of other like-minded people where they live, and past experience has consistently seen misunderstandings, judgement and discrimination. Rebecca's ten-year-old daughter has never asked why they don't date, but she does worry sometimes that her mum is lonely.

Both Rebecca and their daughter are neurodiverse and share an understanding that makes them a tight team. And though Rebecca sometimes wishes there was another adult around for emotional support, company and conversation, they have always found parenting simple.

Sole parents must dig deeper than anyone else could possibly imagine, daily, but without needing to negotiate with another adult who has equal say about their parenting choices. There is the pressure of unbreakable obligation, but there is also no tighter team than single parent and child.

We are so fortunate in our collective of many colours to have the love of chosen family, and for our children to be raised by a veritable rainbow of mops and mamas, babas and dads, aunts, uncles and duncles and all manner of loving looked-up-to figures. Family is so much more than blood; it is that sacred space we take our most ardent hopes and fears, our most unformed parts, and know we will be loved, without condition.

Eamon (he/him) was born in the 1980s to two mums, with some help from a family friend who donated sperm. When Eamon was three his parents split up, and each repartnered with the people they're still with today. As a result, for about as long as he can remember, Eamon has had four mums, along with three new siblings. There weren't a lot of hard-line rules around titles, and Eamon ended up calling all four women mum. It was confusing at times, but ultimately worked well for their family. The original two mums remain close friends, and even lived next door to one another while Eamon was young.

Growing up knowing that family can have many definitions and shades of grey has equipped Eamon with a heart and mind that are open to people and their infinite possibilities.

I THINK THE SINGLE GREATEST GIFT YOU CAN OFFER YOUR CHILD IS TO HELP THEM UNDERSTAND WHO THEY ARE. Give them all the information and let them choose how they feel about it, and what to do with it. Approach these conversations with age-appropriate honesty, an open heart and generous memory, not baulking at the difficult questions, so your children have the chance to form a strong sense of belonging.

Be open with your children about their origin story. Ours know their donor and have an age-appropriate understanding of how they were created. Sometimes our younger child thinks we're talking about donuts – but that's because they're two, and not for any lack of explication. What's never in doubt is how much they are loved, were wanted, and how secure their place is in this world, rooted in the sense of identity and belonging they get from our family and community.

In the world outside your door, the majority of families are mum and dad, plus kid or kids, and this is reflected in literature, television, art, greeting cards and all the rest. **IT'S WORTH SEEKING OUT REPRESENTATION FOR YOUR UNIQUE FAMILY SETUP, NOT ONLY BECAUSE THIS CAN BE EMPOWERING FOR BOTH YOUR CHILDREN AND OTHER CHILDREN TO SEE, BUT BECAUSE IT ALSO ENHANCES THE RICHNESS AND DIVERSITY OF THE WORLD THEY LIVE IN.** If your baby has cousins, you may like to suggest some books to their parents about different forms of family. There are some great titles out there, showing the validity of and love to be found in families with donor-conceived kids, foster kids or adopted kids, blended families, single-parent families and every communion under the sun.

I REMEMBER IN THE DARKEST HOLLOW DAYS OF HOPING AND WISHING FOR OUR BABY THAT MY ARMS FELT SO EMPTY. There are so many people who feel this yearning, and I have always been mindful of their fragile hopes when making any sort of announcement about our babies: that they were growing, that they were born, that they have celebrated a birthday. Always in my heart, along with the joy and pride, is an acknowledgement and respect of the experience of those who have not been as fortunate as us in their journey.

Feelings still crop up that are unexpected. For me, it's when our kids run to their donor and I am, for a moment, keenly aware that I'm the only person in the room who isn't genetically linked to them. I make sure I name those feelings to myself, and later with my partner, and let them go. My children do not share my genetics, but there is no mistaking where they get their silly sense of humour, their tenacity, and their confidence that the best parts of people will emerge when you give them a chance.

My belief is that these feelings only come up because we have been conditioned to think that the only way families are formed is through heteronormative, patriarchal structures and institutions that uphold and perpetuate so much harm. **THE MORE OF US THERE ARE, DEMONSTRATING THAT THERE ARE OTHER WAYS TO LIVE AND LOVE, AND THE MORE VISIBLE OUR FAMILIES BECOME, THE MORE DIVERSE AND PROGRESSIVE THIS WORLD WILL BE.**

Your identity may keep changing and evolving as a parent. Stace (they/them) is a divorced single parent of two daughters. It has only become clear in recent years to them that being asexual is a key part of their identity, coexisting in harmony alongside their non-binary status and role as a mother. Stace wishes for their children to always know they are loved, and to never feel the need to come out regarding any aspect of who they are – that any part of their identity and life is welcome in their family home.

We are all a work in progress, even if you're one hundred years old. And getting to know your children will show you who you are in a way you could never have predicted.

PARENTING IS JUGGLING, LOVE, MESS, ACCEPTANCE, LEVELLING UP. AND DRAWING FROM RESERVES YOU DIDN'T KNOW YOU HAD TO GET THROUGH THE EVER-PRESENT MOMENT. It is long eyelashes resting on a pudgy sleeping face, your arms full of warmth and trust. All we can do is give our best, and forgive ourselves when that doesn't seem like enough.

They are so honest, little children. They have nothing to fear in being just who they are, with no reason for shame or concern for the gaze turned toward them. If you let them, your children will help you feel the same and it can be the most liberating experience of your life.

FINAL THOUGHTS

The love you feel as a parent, the fear and hope and vulnerability and wonder, is exquisite and humbling. Use it to make the best choices you can. The best advice I can offer (other than the naps-before-birth thing) is to always greet your children with joy. When they know you're happy to see them, no matter what, it will help shape such an unshakable sense of self that they'll know their worth in any setting.

And the single greatest gift you can give yourself, next time you look in the mirror, is to regard that person staring back with that same joy and pride and acknowledge that, despite the scars of this world, you are loved. You are worthy. You are here and perfect – as a parent and as a person – just as you are.

THANK YOU

This book would not exist without my generous friend Ailsa Wild, who elevates people and ideas and general joyfulness. Thank you for your trust and your faith in me. That goes for all the peachy keen pals in the wild.

Emily Hart could not have been more enthusiastic and supportive. Em, you are a dream come true in human form and I'm so grateful for all of your work on this book.

Amy Coopes – you disentangled my ideas and laid them out just so, with surgical precision, heart and absolute beauty. Thank you.

Quince Frances, my fave illo and my dear friend, thank you for your vision and your exquisite talent.

Tracey – my wife, my best friend, my home.
Life is good, wild and sweet.

Cathryn, my sister and number one cheerleader, who is such a beautiful mum.

Alex K and Alex C, who helped my breadth of understanding by casting their nets into their fantastic networks. I'm honoured to be in such fine company.

Friends too numerous to mention who offered encouragement and excitement about this book, thank you for the fuel to keep truckin'.

To all of the beautiful families who shared your stories with me, I adore you and it was an honour to get to know you. Our families are amazing. I'm so glad we made this book together and that people like us can walk into a bookstore and pick up a book that resonates, at last.

Published in 2023 by Hardie Grant Books, an imprint of Hardie Grant Publishing

Hardie Grant Books (Melbourne)
Wurundjeri Country
Building 1, 658 Church Street
Richmond, Victoria 3121

Hardie Grant Books (London)
5th & 6th Floors
52–54 Southwark Street
London SE1 1UN

hardiegrantbooks.com

Hardie Grant acknowledges the Traditional Owners of the country on which we work, the Wurundjeri people of the Kulin nation and the Gadigal people of the Eora nation, and recognises their continuing connection to the land, waters and culture. We pay our respects to their Elders past and present.

A catalogue record for this book is available from the National Library of Australia

You'll Be a Wonderful Parent
ISBN 978 1 74379 861 4

10 9 8 7 6 5 4 3 2 1

Design by Amy Daoud
Printed in China by Leo Paper Products LTD.

The paper this book is printed on is from FSC®-certified forests and other sources. FSC® promotes environmentally responsible, socially beneficial and economically viable management of the world's forests.

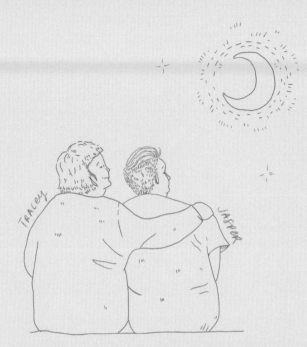

JASPER PEACH lives on stolen Dja Dja Wurrung Country in Castlemaine, Victoria, with their wife and two children. They are a trans, non-binary and disabled writer, editor and broadcaster. They are passionate about equitable access and inclusion, with a strong focus on storytelling centred around the dismantling of misplaced shame. Jasper served as guest co-editor for *Archer Magazine*'s 16th edition, and their work appears in HireUp, *The Sydney Morning Herald*, SBS Voices and *We've Got This*, a book about parenting with a disability.